Ella B. Jenkins™

MEETS

VICE PRESIDENT
KAMALA HARRIS

BY EVE LYNNE AND
WHITNEY JADE GORDY

Hardcover: ISBN 9780983537366-24-99
Softcover: ISBN 9780983537373-4-99
Ebook: ISBN 978-0-9835373-7-3

Library of Congress Control Number: 2020925553

First Paperback Edition December 2020

Edited by Whitney Jade Gordy and Odette Thompson
Cover art concept by Eve Lynne Robinson
Layout by Sofania
Photographs by Eve Lynne Robinson

Printed by Kindle Direct Publishing
and Whitlock Publishing

Robijo Publishing
2318 25 th Ave
Oakland,Ca 94601

Ellabjenkins.com

Dedication

To every first responder and front line worker that
dedicated themselves each day and worked relentlessly
during what has been an unimaginable year.
We dedicate this book to you.

To Madame Vice President Kamala Harris.
Our countries First African-American Female Vice
President.You were our inspiration for creating this story
and our motivation in making certain that this event will
be forever ingrained and immortalized as a
part of American history.

THIS BOOK BELONGS TO

_____

Ella B. Jenkins woke up to a very special Saturday morning. The day was special because she and her family were going on an airplane trip.

Ella's mom was invited to speak at the March on Washington which was being held in a historic park in Washington D.C. People from around the world would be there to support Black Lives Matter and other human rights issues.

Both Ella B. and her baby brother Kingston loved flying on airplanes.

When Ella B.'s family landed in Washington D.C., they were picked up in a large black truck. A man stood outside the truck holding a large sign that read "Jenkins Family".

On the drive to the park, Ella and her family were so happy to see the National Museum of African American History and Culture. They were so excited and exclaimed, "How beautiful!"

15

Ella and her family were thrilled by all of the incredible sights in Washington D.C. While riding in the car, the driver pointed out the Capitol Building to Ella and her family. Ella shouted, "That's the biggest building I have ever seen!"

17

Ella and her family finally arrived at the historic park where everything was happening. Her mom and other guests gave their speeches to an excited crowd of people who had come from many different places.

19

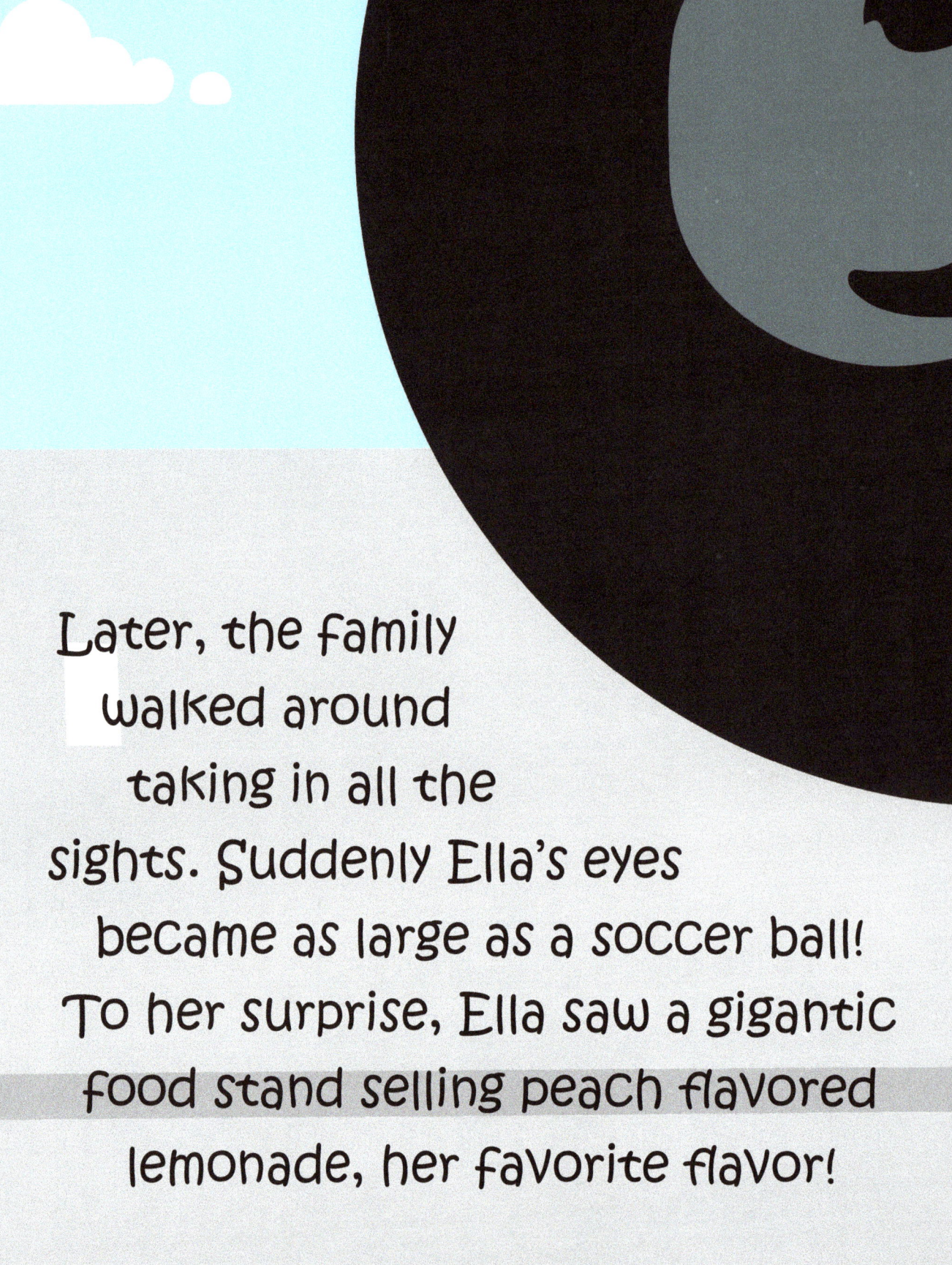

Later, the family
walked around
taking in all the
sights. Suddenly Ella's eyes
became as large as a soccer ball!
To her surprise, Ella saw a gigantic
food stand selling peach flavored
lemonade, her favorite flavor!

21

Ella rushed over and ordered a large peach flavored lemonade. Chef Carmen smiled at her, "That will be thirty-five cents young lady."

As Ella turned around to ask her parents for a dime, she heard a voice behind her offering ten cents. Ella and her family quickly turned around and to their surprise there was Vice President Kamala Harris holding up a shiny dime for Ella.

Ella was overjoyed and asked Vice President Kamala Harris for a hug. She was so excited. Vice President Harris complimented Ella's mom on her fantastic speech and thanked her for her dedication to supporting human rights.

Ella B. told Vice President Kamala Harris, "I am also from Oakland and when I grow up, I hope to be just like you!"

Vice President Kamala Harris told Ella B., "The next time I'm in Oakland, I am going to invite you and your family to take a tour of my office. I want to hear more about your hopes, goals and dreams."

Ella B. looked forward to her plane ride back home. She was going to have so much fun telling her friends about her trip! She couldn't wait to tell them about her meeting Vice President Kamala Harris.

Ella's Back Page

WHY DID ELLA B. WAKE UP SO EXCITED ON THAT VERY SPECIAL SATURDAY MORNING ?

WHAT CITY ARE ELLA B. AND HER FAMILY FLYING TO ?

WHAT IS ELLA B.'S BABY BROTHERS NAME ?

WHY WERE ELLA B. AND HER FAMILY GOING TO WASHINGTON D.C. ?

WHAT COLOR WAS THE TRUCK THAT PICKED UP ELLA B. AND HER FAMILY ?

WHAT IS ELLA B.'S FAVORITE BEVERAGE ?

HOW MUCH MORE MONEY DID ELLA B. NEED TO BUY HER FAVORITE BEVERAGE ?

WHO DID ELLA B. MEET AT THE LEMONADE STAND ?

NAME THE CITY THAT BOTH VICE PRESIDENT KAMALA HARRIS AND ELLA B. WERE BORN IN ?

WHAT QUESTIONS WOULD YOU LIKE TO ASK ELLA B. ?

Did you know?

Washington Monument

Did you know the monument's marble blocks are held together by just gravity and friction?

National Museum of African American History and Culture

Did you know the museum blends design elements that are symbolically African and African American?

Kamala Harris

Did you know Vice President Kamala Harris has been a community activist since she was a child?

At the age of 13, and with her sister's help, Ms. Harris held a demonstration in front of her apartment building to protest the fact that children were not allowed to play on the front lawn. Their efforts were successful and the policy was turned around.

Did you know she was California's first Black woman District Attorney?

Did you know VP Harris is the first HBCU (Historically Black Colleges and Universities) graduate to ever be elected Vice President?

Did you know Vice President Harris was born in Oakland on October 20, 1964, making her the first person born after the 1950s to be elected Vice President?

Kamala Devi Harris
is the current
Vice President
of the United States.

She was born in Oakland, California.

Kamala means "lotus" and is another name for the Hindu goddess Lakshmi—and the empowerment of women.

As a child, Vice President Harris went to both a Black Baptist church and a Hindu temple—embracing both her South Asian and Black identities.

Vice President Harris attended Howard University, the prestigious historically Black college in Washington, D.C. She majored in political science and economics, and joined the Alpha Kappa Alpha (AKA) sorority.

Prior to becoming Vice President, Vice President Harris served as the junior Senator of California and was later elected as the first woman and first Black Attorney General of California.

Vice President Harris is known for her sharp questioning and responses.

Vice President Harris is an enthusiastic cook. Her go-to dinner meal is a simple roast chicken.

Vice President Kamala Harris is the first woman, first African American and first Asian American Vice President in the history of the United States of America.

Eve Lynne

Eve Lynne is a multi-faceted artist.
The *Ella B. Jenkins Meets* series represents
her passion and is a testimony to her life's work
including establishing the Ella B. Jenkins Project
in Nairobi, Kenya and applying her creative vision
to Ella B. Jenkins ceramics, pencils, face masks,
clothing and soon-to-come dolls that children
and adults alike will enjoy.

Whitney Jade Gordy

is a Los Angeles based Licensed marriage and family therapist and trained art therapist. Whitney received her BA in studio arts and MA in Marriage and Family therapy with an emphasis in Clinical Art Therapy from Loyola Marymount University. She spends her time split between working in community based mental health milieus in central Los Angeles and the remainder of her time creating illustrations, paintings and writing short stories. Her surrounding community feeds her passion for holistic methods of self expression and trauma informed healing and self care.

The End

CPSIA information can be obtained
at www.ICGtesting.com
Printed in the USA
LVHW071351071121
702668LV00008B/261